COUNTRY
FLOWERS AND GARDENS

GROWING AND USING FLOWERS, HERBS, AND VEGETABLES

BARBARA RANDOLPH

Friedman Group

A FRIEDMAN GROUP BOOK

Copyright © 1992 by Michael Friedman Publishing Group, Inc.

ISBN 0-517-06116-3

COUNTRY FLOWERS AND GARDENS
was prepared and produced by
Michael Friedman Publishing Group, Inc.
15 West 26th Street
New York, New York 10010

Editor: Robert Hernandez
Art Director: Jeff Batzli
Layout: Charles Donahue
Photography Researcher: Daniella Jo Nilva

Typset by Bookworks Plus
Color separation by Scantrans Pte. Ltd.
Printed in Hong Kong and bound in China by Leefung-Asco Printers Ltd.

To Tim, who has always surrounded our home with country gardens.

© Tim Gibson/Envision

CONTENTS

THE COUNTRY GARDEN

Every country garden has a special feeling, a freedom and exuberance, whether it grows old roses and delphinium, herbs and vegetables, or cutting flowers and ornamental grasses. A country garden isn't pretentious, clipped into fussy hedges, or arranged formally into elaborately shaped beds. And yet some of the world's loveliest country gardens sit in sculptured terraces among the manicured lawns of stately English homes. Within these more formal settings, each bed has the space and freedom that characterize a country garden.

There is no single feature that distinguishes a country garden from all others. It isn't its size, setting, or location. A country garden can flourish in a very small space or a very large one.

A country garden looks as if it had always grown there. It feels part of its surroundings—the buildings, the stone walls, the forests, the landscape, the scenery. Not only is it a delight to look at, it is intended for use: It can be strolled through, or cut and brought indoors for a quick bouquet, or snipped as garnish for a sandwich or a glass of lemonade.

As you wander through the gardens in this book, try to picture each of them in the context of your own land. Consider how you can adapt the ideas here to the one-of-a-kind setting that is yours. A steep, rocky slope is not the place for an herb garden laid out in triangular beds, but the same herbs can grow and thrive just as well arranged casually among the rocks.

In the pages that follow, you'll find gardens for a variety of settings and climates and suggestions for making these plantings work in a good many other environments as well. You can adapt and combine ideas to suit your own taste; you can create a country garden that is uniquely yours.

Remember that wherever you plant flowers, the garden should work with the land. Choose creeping phlox to cascade from the tops of walls and down steep bankings, fistfuls of violets to peek from between the stones in a wall, and tall, dramatic clumps of perennials where you need accent and character. A country garden lets the land suggest the plants that will live there. The country gardener who is sensitive to the land will be rewarded with a beautiful landscape.

A collage of colorful flowers and greenery bring to life even the most colorless of settings.

© Jerry Pavia

Creeping phlox is a good choice for rock gardens or as a ground cover for sloping areas.

PLANNING A GARDEN

Before deciding where to put your garden, you must understand the basic needs of the plants that will grow there. Most garden plants need sunlight and moisture. While some flowers will tolerate shade—and a few woodland flowers thrive in it—nearly all do better with direct sunlight for at least a few hours a day. Choosing the sunniest site for your garden allows you more options in both flowers and vegetables. If the only space available is in the shade, you have two options: You can make the best of it by growing plants suited to that environment, or you can clear the surrounding land of trees to admit more sun.

Although plants need moisture to thrive, very few do well in soggy soil. Avoid marshy areas or low places where water habitually gathers and stays. Plants need water, but most also need good drainage.

When planning which perennial flowers to grow, consider each one's height, since taller plants will often shade lower ones and inhibit their growth. Some plants multiply so quickly that they choke out less vigorous neighbors.

If you are fairly new at gardening, you will most probably be tempted to try to grow everything at once. Each plant you see or smell or read about will interest you, and it may seem impossible to narrow your selection to just a few. It is even harder to choose if you have visited a few well-established gardens and seen how lovely they look with their full clumps and abundant cascades.

The first rule of thumb to remember is that most perennials take a season or two, or even more, to spread into those nicely shaped clumps and mounds. The second is that plants can be moved. Instead of planning a half-acre flower garden, begin with a small layout and alternate spreading perennials with annuals and biennials so there is room for growth but still a good variety of plants.

The same is true for a vegetable plot. Begin small, and don't feel that you must plant every seed in the packet. It is better to have a few plants of each variety than to wear yourself out trying to take care of more than you can handle.

PREPARING THE SOIL

Although sometimes skipped over by hasty gardeners, proper soil preparation is very important to the success of a garden.

Unless you are working in an established garden plot, you will need to remove all grasses, weeds, roots, seedlings, and other growing things from the soil. If you are planting a garden where grass has grown, do *not* rototill the lawn into the soil. Instead, remove the turf (grass and roots) in squares cut with the sharp edge of a spade. By removing the entire growing layer, you prevent existing roots from filling your garden with persistent grass. (You can use the cut blocks of turf to replace a section of poor lawn elsewhere; keep well watered until the turf is established.) To prevent the surrounding lawn from reinvading the plot, use an edging of metal or plastic. Simply push it into the soil along the edges of the bed. Its top should be even with the soil, so it doesn't show.

Once your garden bed is protected from encroachment, prepare the soil by digging it up and loosening it to a depth of six to eight inches. This is easy to do with a spade or a fork. As you work, remove any roots or runners that might remain, and dig out any deep-rooted weeds such as dandelion or chicory (both respected salad greens, but probably unwelcome in your new garden!). Remove rocks, and if your soil is sandy or heavy clay, work in some well-composted manure or other organic material. The ideal soil for most plants contains enough sand for good drainage, but enough organic matter to hold moisture, nutrients, and air.

The ideal soil texture is crumbly and slightly granular, with spaces between the soil particles and the tiny bits of organic matter. When you squeeze a handful of good soil,

A Rototiller loosens soil for planting, but should never be used where grass has grown unless the turf is removed to expose the soil.

© Tim Gibson/Envision

it neither compacts into modeling clay consistency nor runs in a fine stream like sand through your fingers.

The nutrient content of your soil can be determined by a soil test done by your county extension office. The test will tell if your soil is low in any of the three main nutrients (nitrogen, phosphorous, potassium). You can add any of the missing nutrients through a fertilizer rich in those elements. Testing will also tell you the pH balance. The pH can be adjusted by digging in wood ashes (alkaline) or peat moss (acid) around the individual plants.

A little time and energy spent on the soil will repay you amply during many years of gardening. Healthy, weed-free soil not only produces better plants, but it resists disease and new weed growth. Free of underground runners of weed grasses, your soil will grow only those weeds whose seeds land on top of it. These are easy to remove as tiny seedlings.

Most beginning gardeners use perennial plants purchased from nurseries or shared by friends. Although perennials can be raised from seed, they are very slow to establish and often take two years before they are more than spindly, single-stemmed specimens. Save your windowsill space for the seedlings of annual plants.

When purchasing nursery plants, look for those that are healthy and field-grown, if possible. These will be in large pots and have well-developed roots. While smaller greenhouse plants may also do well, field-hardy plants are more suited to the rigors of outdoor life. Some nurseries simply take a shovel into the garden and dig you a clump, while others have pots of field-grown plants already dug up. Either type is ready to plant immediately; freshly dug plants must be replanted at once, before the newly bared rootlets dry out.

When buying tender perennials—those that have been propagated in the greenhouse—look for sturdy plants with strong stems and branches and good root growth. A very gentle tug on the stem right above the soil line will tell you if they have just been potted or if they have a good, developed root system. The risk of losing newly potted plants is much higher, and although you may be willing to try your

Even young children can enjoy helping plants to grow.

luck with one in order to obtain a rare variety, you should be prepared to give it special care.

Tender greenhouse plants will need to "harden off" for about a week before they are planted outside. Water them well and set them outdoors for about two hours in the late afternoon, extending the time for about an hour each day for two or three days, then by two hours a day. Bring them in at night for the first week, then leave them out, still potted, for two nights before transplanting to the garden. Be sure to check them for water on hot, sunny, or windy days; the pots hold very little moisture and the plants shouldn't be allowed to dry out. If it's windy, set the plants in a protected place until they have developed strong stems that won't get damaged.

When the plants have become used to outdoor life, dig holes in the garden about twice the depth and diameter of the pot and mix in some rich humus or potting soil. Fill the hole with water to which you have added a small amount of liquid fertilizer. Stir this rich mud well and make a depression in its center large enough for the roots of your new plant. If it has become pot-bound, tap the pot to loosen its roots slightly, holding the plant over the hole so any loose potting soil will fall in.

The best time to transplant is on a cloudy, fairly warm day, when plants will suffer the least shock. On a sunny day, transplant late in the afternoon or very early in the morning. Check the plants during the hottest part of the first few days, giving them a little shade if necessary.

Annual plants may be purchased in flats or grown from seeds.

Separate pots allow each seedling to grow without interference from others.

STARTING ANNUALS
FROM SEED

If you have a sunny window or a glassed-in porch on the sunny side of the house, you might enjoy growing at least some of your annual plants from seed.

Start the seeds in long plastic trays divided into inch-wide rows, and set in deeper solid plastic trays that hold water. Or, if you are starting only a few plants, use individual peat pots or small flowerpots. Use a sterile starting medium—such as Jiffy-Mix—that is fine and light in texture and can hold necessary moisture without becoming soggy and drowning tiny sprouts. A fine-grained starter mix also makes it easier to separate the tender roots and move them to individual pots later.

Pour the dry soil mix into the long trays, filling each to within one-quarter inch of the top. Shake the trays gently to settle, but not pack, the mix, then add more if needed. Tap the seeds gently onto the soil, trying to avoid clumping, and spread with your fingers until there are about eight to ten to the inch or three or four to a pot. Some seeds are so

This leafy annual is ready for planting.

tiny, it is almost impossible to get them evenly spread, so don't fuss.

To meet the lighting needs of each type of plant—read the packets carefully to learn what these are—cover the seeds with as much as one-half inch of starter mix. Set the seed trays into solid trays half-filled with lukewarm water. Be sure to label each section so you can tell the seedlings apart when they sprout. Set the trays in a warm place where they will get as much sun as possible.

When the seedlings are about one inch tall, transfer them to individual pots, carefully separating the roots. Put two or three in each pot, unless the seeds are very precious or the germination is poor. In these instances, it is better to use a single pot for a weak seedling than to lose a possible plant. When plants are well started and have developed true leaves, cut off all but the strongest plant in each pot, clipping with scissors instead of pulling, to avoid disturbing the roots of the remaining plant.

By the time they are well established in individual pots, these annuals may be hardened off and planted into the garden whenever the weather conditions are right, just as you would purchased plants.

Once plants are established in the garden, they are quite easy to care for. Weeds can be removed easily if they are pulled before they have a chance to develop deep or pervasive roots.

PROTECTING PLANTS
IN WINTER

Many perennials die back to ground level each winter, springing up again the following year with no particular effort on your part. But others, such as lavender, retain woody growth over the winter, and form new leaves on these existing plants in the spring. If left untrimmed, woody stems are likely to form new spring growth at their outer tips, leaving bare, straggly center stems. These plants should be pruned back in the fall, but not so far back as to remove all the leaves, which continue to support the plant until it is completely dormant.

Black plastic helps keep rows weed-free during the growing season, but should not be used as winter mulch.

Plastic cones provide protection for roses, both as insulation and support against the weight of the snow.

The root systems of such plants are fairly fragile, and the alternate freezing and thawing of the ground breaks the tiny root hairs that channel nourishment and moisture to the plant in the spring. To prevent root damage, mulch woody plants lightly with a layer of pine boughs or salt hay or straw once the ground has frozen. (Don't use stable straw; the last thing your plants need as they enter winter is a high-nitrogen fertilizer.) Leaves are not a good mulch, since they pack down and hold too much moisture, which can damage the roots. Some gardeners fear that pine needles will add acidity to the soil, but this is not the case. Pine trees thrive in acid soil and tend to grow there, but they do not make the soil acidic with their needles. In any event, the branches will be removed, and the ground raked in the spring before the needles will have a chance to compost into the soil.

Before the vegetation on nonwoody perennials dies back to the ground, mark their locations with sticks or other durable markers. Markers will help you avoid digging up the plants by mistake in the spring as you clean out the beds for early planting.

In the spring, remove the mulch from woody perennials as the ground begins to thaw—about the time the first tulip leaves emerge. Clean up the perennial beds and tidy up any unwanted spreading growth in preparation for the new season.

While annual plants do not need winter protection, they do need some attention before they are left for the winter. As plants stop producing or are blackened by frost, pull them up by the roots. Remove these dead plants from the garden so that any disease or hardy insect will not be able to lie in wait for next year's crops.

© Gail Meese/Envision

This established lawn can survive a dry year. It will be green again after a rainy spring.

COPING WITH DROUGHT

1. Use a soaker hose to water slowly and deeply directly into the soil. Sprinklers may cover a broader area at one time, but a great deal of their water is lost to evaporation in the air and on plant foliage. Spraying also waters the area between rows and encourages weeds to grow, taking precious water away from plants.

2. Mulch with organic material, such as straw or shredded bark, to keep moisture in the soil. Black plastic holds in water, but it also holds in heat, which may damage roots if severe drought accompanies a heat wave.

3. Use shade netting to protect plants from direct sun. While plants need sunlight for growth, scorching sun causes them to shrivel and use up more water. By shading lightly during the hottest part of the day, you can prevent this trauma and allow the plants to make more efficient use of the moisture they have.

4. Protect plants from the drying effects of wind with netting or windbreaks. A windbreak can be as simple as brush piled against the garden fence on the side of the prevailing wind.

5. Water plants in the evening, especially if you must use a spray system, to prevent evaporation and to cut down the shock of cold water on hot, sun-drenched plants.

6. Water plants thoroughly twice a week, instead of daily. Water will have a chance to soak downward into the root area where it's needed. Shallow watering encourages roots to grow upward in search of surface water and subjects them to even more damage when the ground dries out.

7. Water the most precious and the least drought-resistant plants first. Lawns, especially established ones, can withstand a dry year; they may turn brown but will not be lost. Juicy vegetables, such as cucumbers, tomatoes, and melons, need the most water. Root vegetables are able to go deeper into the soil for moisture.

8. Use water from the bathtub for watering the garden. If you are recycling bathwater, be sure not to use bath oils or bubble bath products. A little soap, however, is actually good for plants by keeping soft-bodied insects off the leaves.

9. If you must set out new plants during a drought, do so in the evening and mix plenty of organic material into the soil to retain moisture.

AN HERB GARDEN

Herbs are among the most rewarding and useful plants—attractive in the garden, tasty on the table, and fragrant and decorative in the kitchen. Except for mint, most culinary herbs remain tidy and attractive in the garden. Once established, they withstand drought, poor soil, blazing sun, and inattention. They thrive with tender loving care, but they will survive without it.

Even in a country setting, herbs lend themselves to little garden plots where varieties can be kept separate. Herb beds are often planted in shapes—square, with diagonally crossed paths, or round, with radiating wedge-shaped beds.

You can plant an herb garden from seed, but seedlings require careful tending and patience and provide few perennial plants large enough for use in the first year. Most gardeners begin with a few sturdy nursery plants that will provide attractive growth and a harvest the first season.

Because so many herbs grow natively in the sparse, lean soil of the dry Mediterranean hillsides, a myth has gained acceptance that herbs actually do best in these conditions. The fact is that, like any other plant, herbs will respond best when treated well. It is true that overfertilizing causes many of them to produce less flavorful leaves, but good growing conditions in moderately loamy soil will produce fragrant, flavorful herbs that are also healthy plants and attractive in the garden.

The easiest herb bed to build and plant is a simple square bisected by two diagonal paths. This plan forms four triangles and provides easy access to all parts of the bed. Each triangle offers ample space for at least four plants. Put a

Beebalm makes a good background plant, since it is taller than many other herbs.

tall or spreading perennial in the center of each, an annual or biennial at each of the center corners, and smaller perennials at the outside corners.

Thyme, lavender, mint (in a large sunken pot), lemon balm, beebalm, or chive are good center choices. Tarragon, winter savory, scented geranium, salad burnet, small sages, rosemary (except in the South, where it grows quite large), oregano, lamb's ears, or chamomile are good plants for the outside corners. If the garden is fairly small, the

center plants may soon fill the beds, at which time you stop planting the annuals. You can either prune back the roots of the center plants to make room for the more upright corner perennials, or you can move them to another garden.

Tall or rapidly spreading plants such as yarrow, artemisia, and tansy are not appropriate unless the beds are quite large. If you begin with a small square, other identical gardens can be added, either in a row or forming a larger square made up of four smaller ones.

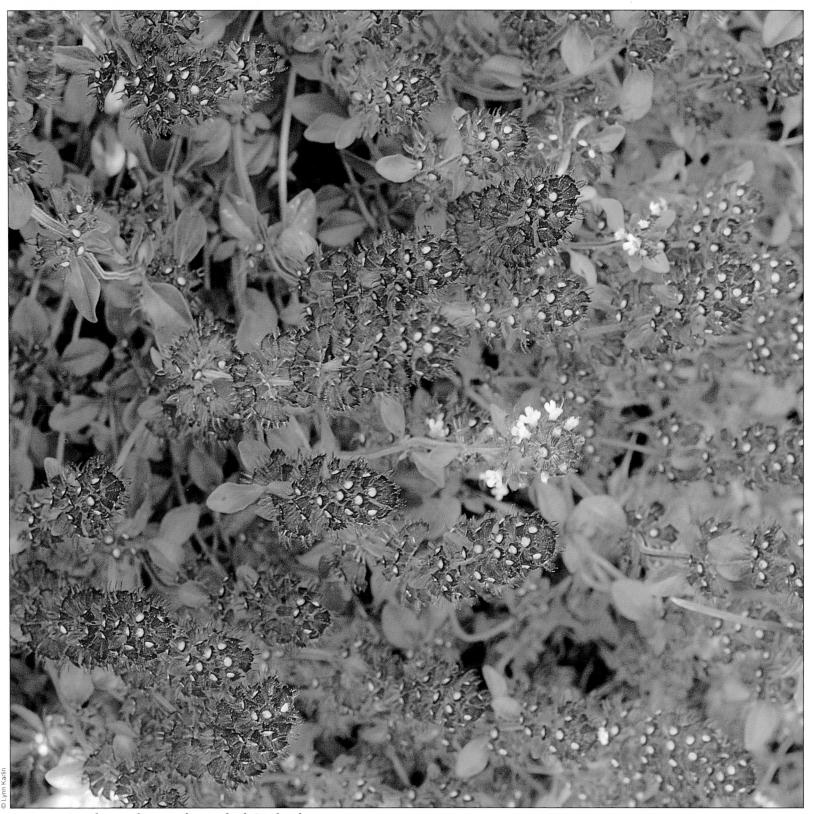

© Lynn Karlin

Low-growing thyme plants make good edging borders.

Herbs are perfect plants for small, separated beds.

© Joanne Pavia

Larger gardens often have a focal point such as a sundial, statue, bee skep, bench, or arbor, either in the center or at one end. A potted bay or rosemary can serve the same purpose, giving a dimension of height, as can a raised bed filled with tall artemisia or yarrow planted in the center of a larger square.

Many herb gardens are developed around a special theme and display herbs associated with a hobby or interest. Biblical, historical, potpourri, and tea gardens are possibilities. Gardeners of literary bent might want to plant herbs mentioned by poets or referred to by Shakespeare. If you have a porch or patio where you sit on a summer evening, you might surround it with a moonlight garden of pale green and gray foliage and white flowers.

A tea garden could be planted in mints, beebalm, catnip, chamomile, sage, costmary, and scented geraniums. It might contain a bench or a tiny iron patio table and chairs, just large enough for teatime. In this garden, you could add an arbor of climbing roses and a border of nasturtiums for your tea sandwiches.

A biblical garden could include those plants mentioned in the Bible or those known to grow in the Holy Land today. Or you might grow those herbs associated with the Virgin Mary or other saints. Rosemary, costmary, lady's-mantle, lady's bedstraw, and calendula (pot marigold) were all named for Mary, while lavender, bay, chive, horehound, rose, violet, sage, woodruff, tansy, and thyme have all been associated with saints or Christian observance.

HERBS TO GROW

BASIL is a fast-growing annual that often reaches a height of twenty-four inches. Used in salads, with tomatoes, and in pesto, it is a favorite of Italian cooks. If you plan to use basil for pesto, plant several, since one batch can take an entire plant. Pinch off the flowering stems to encourage better leaf growth. Be sure to protect basil at the first hint of frost, since it is the most sensitive of all garden plants. Bush basil and purple varieties are smaller and good choices for limited spaces.

© Lynn Karlin

Calendula, or pot marigold, provides showy blooms all summer if the blossoms are picked off as they begin to fade.

The compact habits of most herbs make them good neighbors in the garden.

BEEBALM is a tall, stately perennial with red, pink, or white blossoms. Use its fragrant, buttonlike dried heads in arrangements and wreaths, and its fresh or dried leaves for the distinctive flavor of Earl Grey tea blends. Allow it room to spread in the garden.

CHIVE, a perennial of the onion family, spreads quickly into attractive clumps. Use it in salads or with eggs, potatoes, or cottage cheese to add a delicate onion flavor. The pink blossoms are good in salads or scrambled eggs. Chive grows twelve to eighteen inches tall and makes an attractive border behind other plants. The garlic chive variety has flat leaves, white flowers, and a distinctive garlic flavor.

DILL is an annual, three to four feet tall, that is usually planted in a clump so its long stems can support each other. It is better grown from seed, since its short, fragile roots often don't survive transplanting. Rake an area one to three feet square and scatter the seeds generously. Rake again, or sprinkle with soil, and keep well watered until the seedlings are strong. Dill leaves are good with fish or new potatoes, and seed heads are used in pickling and in rye bread. If you leave a few heads to mature and dry in the garden, they are likely to self-sow next year's crop.

MARJORAM is a versatile perennial used with meats, in salads, and in Italian and Greek dishes. Since there are several varieties, not all of them flavorful, ask if you can taste a leaf before purchasing a plant. If it doesn't have a clear flavor, it is not a culinary variety. Don't blame the nursery, however, since the varieties don't always run true and the labeling on seeds is often unclear. The nonculinary variety has lovely magenta flowers that dry very well for everlasting arrangements.

© Joanne Pavia

Dill grows taller than most herbs, so is best grown in the vegetable garden or in the background of an herb border.

MINT is best known for its pervasive habits. The perennial, often two to three feet tall, spreads so quickly that it can easily take over a small garden, or even a lawn. Plant it in a large metal tub or bucket, sunk right to its rim in the garden. Or, better yet, plant it at the edge of a field where it doesn't matter if it does spread. Use mint in cold drinks, in salads, and for making jelly.

PARSLEY is one of the few biennial herbs. It grows about twelve inches high. Plants will come back a second year and go quickly to seed; the subsequent leaves are small and tough, so begin with new plants each spring. Three to six plants should provide enough of this herb, which is used as garnish and to counter the aftertaste of garlic. Of the two varieties, curly and Italian, the latter has better flavor and texture.

SALAD BURNET is a perennial herb used in salads for its distinct cucumber flavor. It grows up to twelve inches tall in a neat mound that remains green until snow covers it.

The deep green color of parsley is a nice contrast to the gray-green foliage of many other herbs.

Mint spreads quickly and is best planted away from other herbs, or it will soon overwhelm them.

© Robert E. Lyons

Sage is an easy-to-grow perennial that can be used fresh or dried for cooking.

The best time to harvest thyme for culinary use is before it blooms.

SAGE is a fairly hardy perennial that can grow to a small shrub in a few years, so be sure to leave it plenty of room. It is used with chicken and veal and in sausage. Trim it fairly close to the main stem when cutting it in the fall, since it will die back anyway and close cutting makes it bushier the following year.

TARRAGON is a hardy perennial, growing to thirty inches in good soil. Be sure to get French tarragon, since the Russian variety has the flavor of stale grass clippings and grows rangy and tall, eventually taking over the entire garden. Use tarragon with fish or chicken. Plants should be dug up and divided every three years or they will become root-bound.

THYME is a low-growing perennial with many varieties. Those often sold as French or English are the best for general use. All grow in tidy clumps that expand outward each year as their branches touch the ground and take root. Use in soups and stews or with lamb, chicken, or pork.

Chive blossoms in a garden attract bees.

HARVESTING

Throughout their growing season, herbs can be harvested regularly. Even as fairly small plants, snipping a few sprigs or leaves for cooking keeps the plant trim and tidy and encourages fuller growth. For larger harvests of herbs to preserve for winter use, the best time is just before the plant blooms, since the oils that give flavor and fragrance to the leaves are most concentrated then.

Perennial herbs grown in beds should be harvested evenly, so that plants retain their shape. Annuals, such as basil and summer savory, can be harvested frequently by picking off the tops. This encourages the plants to grow bushier and send out side branches, as well as delays blossoming. Plants whose leaves grow from a central root crown, such as salad burnet, should be picked by cutting each stem close to the ground. Chives should be harvested in the same way, with each sprig cut close to its base.

To keep harvested herbs fresh, put them in a vase of water or, in the case of parsley, chervil, and coriander, wrap loosely in a damp paper towel and store in a plastic bag in the refrigerator. Fresh herbs purchased at a farm stand or grocer's should be placed in water immediately or stored in the refrigerator in damp paper towels. If you grow your own, pick each day's supply as needed.

Harvest herbs for drying in the morning, after the dew has dried, but before the midday heat sets in. Tie stems in bunches and hang in a shaded, airy place. You can suspend bunches inside large paper bags to protect leaves from dust. Bags also catch dried leaves that fall off.

When the herbs are dry, the leaves can be stripped from the stems and stored in glass jars. Although dry herbs can be left hanging, they stay cleaner in a container.

Chives and dill do not dry well, and basil and parsley often turn brown when dried. Freezing preserves both color and flavor in these herbs if you pack them tightly in plastic bags with as little air space as possible. To use, simply shave off the needed amount, which will thaw instantly into green, fresh-looking chopped herbs.

Vinegars are another way of preserving fresh herb flavors. The rich herb flavors permeate the vinegar, which can be used to flavor salad dressings and marinades. Use red wine vinegar with any herb you would use in salads: basil, marjoram, oregano, salad burnet, chives, dill, mint, or any blend of these. Fill a jar about a third full of herbs, then fill with vinegar, seal, and store in a shady place for two weeks. Mint preserved in cider vinegar is especially good on roast lamb. Use white wine vinegar for tarragon and white distilled vinegar for lemon balm or chive blossoms. Purple basil turns white distilled vinegar a lovely lavender color.

DRYING HERBS IN A MICROWAVE OVEN

Each oven has its own settings, so you will have to experiment a little with your own. Wash and pat herbs as dry as possible. Fold fresh herb sprigs in a layer of paper towel and microwave on high for thirty seconds. Check the herbs and continue to microwave in thirty-second intervals until they begin to dry a little, then at fifteen-second intervals until they are crisp. Seal in jars immediately. Herbs dried in a microwave usually retain their color and shape better than air-dried plants.

Marjoram dries well as a flavoring for winter soups and salads.

The pink color of chive blossoms lasts for a long time when they are dried for ornamental use.

© Joanne Pavia

CHAPTER THREE

A VEGETABLE GARDEN

To anyone who loves good food, there is no substitute for fresh-picked produce. The green beans are snappier, the tomatoes sweeter, the corn more tender. The vegetable gardener can, moreover, choose varieties on the basis of flavor, not how well they ship or how long they stay looking fresh on the grocer's shelf. There are no special secrets to a vegetable garden, but if you follow a few general practices, you can help it to grow better and faster. Begin by planting only as much as you can handle. A small, well-tended garden will produce more than a larger garden gone to neglect.

Clearing land of weeds and roots before you plant makes a garden much easier to keep weed-free later. If your soil is sandy, enrich it with compost or other organic material and dig it in well. Be sure you have a source of water if summer drought is a problem. Fence your garden if it is close to the woods or in a wild area. Mowing a wide swath around it will also help discourage small animals from marauding it while you sleep.

Planting times vary with each climate and terrain; the best way to find out when to plant different vegetables in your area is to ask a gardening neighbor or your local county extension office. In general, root crops, peas, and early greens are planted as soon as the ground can be worked. Squash, cucumber, and other fast-growing but frost-sensitive vegetables are planted about two weeks before the last expected frost. Vegetables started indoors or in greenhouses are set out into the garden only after the danger of frost is past. In southern and central states, many vegetables can be planted directly in the garden, while in the North those same vegetables must be started indoors in order to mature during the short growing season.

Most gardeners prefer to plant in a traditional pattern of rows. Sometimes two rows are planted quite close with a wider space between each pair of rows. Double rows use space more efficiently, but still allow the gardener enough room to reach the plants easily. They work well for medium-sized compact plants such as peppers, broccoli, and green beans. Crops such as carrots, beets, radishes, and loose salad greens work well in wide rows, where seeds are scattered in an area about twelve inches wide. As plants sprout, they can be thinned to the distance directed on the seed package.

For most of us, the reward of gardening is in the harvest. To make the best of all the work, it is important to know just when to pick each vegetable. Bigger isn't always better, and most vegetables are the most tender, sweet, and delicious when they are picked quite small. There is no comparison, for example, between a succulent, tender zucchini, hardly larger than your thumb, and the tough, tasteless baseball bats of a week or so later.

Leaf lettuces provide one of the garden's earliest crops in the spring.

In order to grow healthy beets, the seedlings should be thinned to a few inches apart.

A full basket of greens and vegetables fresh from the garden is the reward of a summer's work.

Peas should be picked when they are firm and round inside, but while the pods are still firm and deep green. As the pod matures, the peas lose their flavor as well as their tender texture. Green beans are tender and flavorful while pencil-sized and should barely begin to show the bumps of the seeds inside.

You will soon begin to recognize each vegetable at its own peak of perfection. Picking young vegetables encourages new ones to grow, whereas leaving them on the vine to mature causes the plant to stop producing. Use or refrigerate vegetables soon after picking to retain flavor and nutrients.

READING THE SEED CATALOG

Seed catalogs, except for the few designed especially for regional gardeners, are intended to be used by gardeners from Nova Scotia to Texas. When you shop from a catalog, it is important to look for crops that will perform well in your own climate. Varieties labeled "drought resistant" may be right for the Southwest, "slow to bolt" for the South, and "early producing" for the North. Experimental gardens all over the continent are busy breeding vegetables for all climates, so take advantage of their research and choose the best seeds for your region.

While most seed packets contain far more seeds than are needed for a family garden, some seed catalogs cater to the small gardener who needs only a few plants of each variety. Shepherd's Garden Seeds, for example, offers a single packet with a fine selection of different salad greens and another with an assortment of hot peppers.

Seed catalogs are often packed with information, not only on the varieties, but on gardening as well. Johnny's Selected Seeds publishes such a catalog; you can learn a lot about gardening just from reading it.

Peppers grow best where temperatures remain warm at night.

Peas are a cool-weather crop that should be planted very early in the spring.

Carrots grow best in sandy soil. Lighten a heavy soil with sandy loam before planting.

VEGETABLES TO GROW

BROCCOLI grows well in the North, yielding an especially abundant harvest if you choose varieties that produce secondary side shoots after the main head has been picked. Be sure to harvest while the florets are tight and deep green, before they have overbloomed.

CARROTS have the advantage of a long harvest. Plant seeds a few inches apart, directly in the garden, early in the spring. Harvest sweet baby carrots early, large carrots in the fall.

CHINESE GREENS are among the special joys of a home garden, since many varieties are hard to find. These "cut and come again" vegetables continue to produce from a few plants. They vary from mildly aromatic to quite pungent. Most do best in the cooler weather of spring and fall and should be harvested before they are overgrown, since most bolt (go to seed) quite quickly.

CHINESE PEAS are grown for the whole pods, which can be eaten raw or stir-fried. The dwarf varieties are best for munching raw, while mammoth varieties freeze well. Like English peas, these need to be planted early and harvested daily.

CORN tastes dramatically different when eaten fresh from the garden. In New England, there's an old saying that you don't pick the corn until the pot's boiling. But corn does require space and is not the right crop for a little kitchen garden. Plant it in a block of several short rows, side by side instead of one long row.

CUCUMBERS can be planted directly in the garden or started indoors for earlier yield. The vines grow quickly and need plenty of space to ramble. Choose slicing varieties for salads and sliced pickles, smaller pickling varieties for dills and gherkins. Cucumbers need a lot of water and

Broccoli should be picked when the heads are tight and deep green.

should be picked before they become fat or even slightly yellow. To water cucumbers in a dry climate, plant them around a gallon plastic milk jug that is pierced with holes. Leave the neck of the jug above ground and fill it daily from the garden hose. The water seeps into the ground, giving the roots the moisture they need to produce high-quality cucumbers.

ENGLISH PEAS are easy to grow, especially in the North. Plant them very early so they can mature before the hot weather sets in. They need a wire fence to climb on and should be harvested daily since they become overgrown very quickly. Among the first vegetables to harvest, English peas are also among the easiest and most reliable to freeze.

PEPPERS come in such an enormous variety of sizes, colors, and flavors that it would be possible to plant a whole row with no two the same. All have similar growth habits. Peppers need warmth in order to blossom, so a mulch of black plastic is a good idea in the North. Lay a plastic sheet along the row, bury its edges, and cut holes for plants about a foot apart. Peppers do best if the leaves of neighboring plants are touching slightly. They are usually started indoors or purchased from nurseries to give a longer growing season.

PUMPKINS are great for the gardener with lots of room. No crop will bring you more friends among the neighborhood children than a patch of glowing orange pumpkins. Plant large varieties for jack-o'-lanterns and sweet small pumpkins for pies. Be prepared to give the

sprawling vines a lot of space, or plant the new bush varieties.

RADISHES, either the round red ones or the peppery white icicle varieties, enliven salad and relish trays. Easy to grow and early to harvest, a continuous crop is easily maintained if you drop a seed in the hole each time you pick a radish. Don't plant too many at once, since they are quick to bolt.

SNAP BEANS come in green, wax, or purple varieties (the latter turn green when cooked). Pole, or climbing, beans take up less garden space and are easier to harvest, but bush beans survive early fall frosts better. Choose stringless varieties and pick beans when they are still very small and tender.

Winter squash varieties can be harvested late in the fall and stored for several months.

Hot peppers add zest to foods while they are fresh, or may be dried by hanging them in bunches.

TOMATOES are everyone's favorite fresh garden vegetables, perhaps because the difference between fresh-picked and shipped tomatoes is so obvious. Choose round varieties for eating, plum or Italian types for sauces. Be sure they have plenty of fertilizer, and keep them well watered. Tomatoes are usually started indoors or bought as nursery plants for longer yield.

OLD-FASHIONED VEGETABLES

While vegetables may not go out of style as fast as rock groups and hemlines, they are still subject to the whims of fashion. Grocers' shelves are full of a wide variety our grandparents never saw, but our grandparents grew and loved a number of vegetables that are rarely found today in supermarkets *or* gardens. Fortunately, many of the seeds for old-fashioned varieties are still available, although they are sometimes hard to find.

Some of these forgotten vegetables are among the easiest to grow. Kohlrabi is a good example. Once a staple of New England gardens, it is now a curiosity when found on the "gourmet" vegetable shelf. How our great grandmothers would laugh to see it there! Kohlrabi is a member of the cabbage family, whose main stem enlarges into a bulb just above the ground. Its leaves stick out all over it on short stems, and it looks like no other vegetable on earth. It is planted early in the spring and is best sown at one week intervals to provide a continuous crop. Kohlrabi grows fairly quickly in cold weather. Thin to about four inches apart when the plants are about three inches tall; you can use the thinnings sliced raw in salads or stir-fried.

Harvest kohlrabis when they are about the size of golf balls, and boil them whole and unpeeled. The top leaves can be added at the last minute. Let a few grow until they are about three inches in diameter and hollow out the centers using a melon baller. Parboil them a few minutes and stuff with ground pork or veal that has been sautéed and mixed with some bread crumbs, a little thyme, and an egg. Bake them until they are tender but not mushy.

Kohlrabi should be harvested when it is no larger than a golf ball.

Swiss chard and kale should be in every beginner's garden, just because they are so encouraging. They grow quickly and abundantly and look so nice in the garden that they give the novice a great sense of success. Neither one goes to seed, and one planting will provide.results all summer. Simply keep harvesting the outer stalks of chard and the bottom leaves of kale.

Try cooking chard as the Swiss do, separating the stalks and leaves. Boil or steam the stalks and serve in a light cream sauce. Steam the chopped leaves and serve as a sepa-rate dish with a touch of butter and a dash of vinegar. Kale can also be used all summer, either as a cooked green or cut into thin strips to add color, flavor, and nutrients to soups. Its flavor improves after the first heavy frost. When the rest of the garden is a memory, it is still deep green and delicious. That's the time to make a hearty soup of kale with beef broth, potatoes, onions, and sliced smoked sausage.

Salsify is so nearly forgotten that few garden books even mention it. Sow it early in the spring and thin to seven or eight inches apart when it is about three inches tall. It will

© Joanne Pavia

Green kale (not the ornamental varieties) is the basis of a classic Portuguese soup.

withstand drought and is shunned by pests, so your crop has a good chance of making it to harvest in October. Dig up the roots, scrape them, and boil in water to which a little vinegar has been added. A favorite way of serving salsify was baked in a casserole mixed with bread crumbs and butter; or they were parboiled, then rolled in egg and bread crumbs before deep frying. In either case, they were so often described as tasting like oysters that they were known as "vegetable oysters."

Parsnips must be the world's most misunderstood vegetables. They would never have gone out of style if everyone had kept picking them fresh from the garden. The woody, tasteless remnants of them that are found in the grocery store are a sorry substitute for their sweet tender fresh roots.

Parsnips require patience to grow, since they are not harvested until they have spent the winter frozen under the snow. Prepare the soil as deep as you would for carrots and plant the seeds in April. Plant thickly and use all the seeds, since germination is often poor and the seeds won't keep until next year. Thin to about four inches apart. Be sure to avoid the plants if you plow in the fall; dig them as soon as the ground thaws in the spring. Slice and boil or stir-fry with a slice of gingerroot, and serve with plenty of butter.

The Jerusalem artichoke—also called the "sunchoke"—is really a perennial sunflower. It resembles a small, lumpy potato and has a crispy texture that is not lost with cooking. Don't plant it in your flower bed, even though its yellow flowers are very attractive, since it will take over very quickly. Plant it alongside the barn or a shed, where its tall stems will have some support. Plant in the spring and you should be able to dig a few the first fall. They don't store well, so dig only what you need for a few days at a time. Always leave enough to keep the bed growing. Slice the roots raw in salads, boil whole, or roast with lamb, pork, or beef.

The Jerusalem artichoke is a member of the sunflower family.

© Lynn Karlin

Zucchini blossoms are a favorite food in Italy.

ZUCCHINI SURPLUS? NIP IT IN THE BUD

If you wonder how to stem the tide of zucchini that floods your garden from only a few plants, you can literally nip it in the bud! The blossoms are a delicious vegetable in their own right, providing you with innovative dinners and a clear conscience.

The American Indians were probably the first to try the flowers as food; the Zuni of the Southwest fried them separately and also used them to flavor other dishes. Although they are now a great favorite in the cuisines of many European countries, the squash is an indigenous American vegetable.

To harvest the blossoms, clip them with scissors just as they are about to open. Although the male blossoms (those with the long thin stems) are larger and easier to use for some dishes, the female blossoms (the ones with little squashes beginning to form at the base) are just as tasty. If zucchini population control is not your purpose, use the male blossoms. If you use female blossoms, clip out the pistil in the center of the flower and clip the stems as close as possible on all blossoms.

If you don't plan to use the blossoms immediately, place them in a plastic bag and seal it closed, including a lot of air space, like a balloon. The air cushion will protect the blossoms in the refrigerator. Wash them very carefully just before you use them and drain on paper towels. They are very fragile, so it is best not to pile them in layers when you harvest or put them in storage.

Stuffed squash blossoms are a good main dish, and are a perfect use for leftover chicken, ham, or any other meat. Add a few slivers of salami or pepperoni for extra flavor.

SAUSAGE STUFFING

1 pound Italian sausage

½ cup chopped onion

½ cup chopped green or sweet red pepper

3 cloves garlic (or to taste)

1 tablespoon olive oil

½ cup fresh grated Parmesan cheese

½ cup coarse, fresh bread crumbs

Sauté sausage, onion, pepper, and garlic in oil in a skillet until sausage is cooked. Drain well (spread on paper towels to remove even more fat if preferred). Add cheese and bread crumbs and mix well, adding the oil if necessary to hold it together slightly. Place about a tablespoonful in the center of each blossom and close, twisting ends together or folding them underneath.

Bake in a buttered baking dish at 300°F for about half an hour.

Makes 30 squash blossoms.

From this basic mixture, you can create an endless variety of stuffings. Substitute chopped chicken, ham, lamb, or any other cooked meat, and add after the peppers and onions have been sautéed in a little oil. Omit peppers entirely for a more subtle flavor, or substitute Mexican varieties for a more piquant one.

Add other sautéed vegetables, such as chopped baby zucchini, and add herbs such as tarragon, basil, or marjoram if you are not using sausage for flavoring. Try nearly any cheese in place of Parmesan, such as fontina, feta, or a soft cheese like ricotta.

Frying in batter is a favorite Italian use for squash blossoms, as is sautéeing lightly in olive oil or butter. To sauté, use buds that are still closed. These make a nice topping for delicately flavored pastas and a superb filling for a breakfast or luncheon omelet.

The batters for frying blossoms can be as easy or as simple as you like. Use the same batter that you use for tempura, or make a simple one of three eggs and one-half cup flour. This makes a thick batter perfect for sautéeing the blossoms in butter. Simply dip each blossom into the batter and fry until lightly browned on each side.

BLOSSOM FRITTERS

2 cups flour

1 tablespoon baking powder

1 teaspoon sugar

1 egg

¼ cup milk

½ cup water

2 cups coarsely chopped squash blossoms

cooking oil for deep frying

Blend dry ingredients. Blend egg, milk, and water and add to dry mixture. Beat until smooth, and add blossoms. Heat ½ inch of oil in skillet to a temperature of about 360°F and drop batter by teaspoonful into hot oil. Cook two or three minutes on each side until golden brown. Remove and drain. Serve hot.

Makes 4 appetizer servings.

Because so many people are growing squash just for the blossoms, one seed house has developed a squash that has especially abundant and large male blooms. Called Butterblossom, it also produces an excellent zucchini-type squash if the female blossoms are left to mature.

© Jerry Pavia

CHAPTER FOUR

A FRAGRANT GARDEN

Planting a garden especially for fragrance was a popular pastime of Victorians, a delightful custom that deserves revival. In an olitory (the name for such a garden), plants should be placed within easy reach, since many release their fragrance only when the foliage is brushed against or moved to activate the fragrant oils. Such a garden could be used as a border atop a retaining wall or terrace, where it would be easy to bury your nose in the plants without bending over.

A potpourri garden of scented herbs could have an old-fashioned June-blooming rosebush in the center, or a central bed could be circular and planted to look like a nosegay or tussy-mussy. Tufts of clove pink bordered in white-edged silver thyme will give the appearance of lace surrounding rosebuds. Sweet and spicy plants such as rosemary, lemon verbena, scented geraniums, mints, lemon grass, lemon balm, lavender, chamomile, and bay make fragrant additions to this garden.

Try to make room for a bench where you can pause for a moment to enjoy the aromas. Such a scented corner might be set against a banking, with fragrant flowers growing at nose level behind the bench or roses planted at each end of it. A sweet-smelling shrub, such as mock orange or an arbor behind or over the bench, could offer some shade.

In choosing plants, look for a variety of scents, not just the sweet heavy ones. Lemon verbena and lavender are invigorating, while lemon balm and chamomile are soothing. Plant chamomile and woolly thyme between the paving stones. Clove pinks add a spicy fragrance, and scented geraniums can be set in pots that can be brought indoors for winter.

Fragrant plants lining a walkway release their scent whenever someone brushes past them.

Although a scented garden, especially if it is planted atop a wall, can be a simple border, you can also use a more formal plan. If you have a bench at one end, you could use a very old design called a "goosefoot." Actually, it looks more like a fan, with a series of wedge-shaped beds radiating from a single point to form a semicircle. This same design is also good for a garden that lies with one side against a wall or arbor.

A circle within a square is an attractive arrangement. Beds are laid out much as in the simple square herb garden (see page 25), but the center is a circular bed with a path around it. This center bed gives you the luxury of a showy focal point. Tall plants such as beebalm could be grown there, or a large pot of bay or rosemary could be placed there and taken indoors in the winter. In kinder climates, where these plants winter over outdoors, they can be planted directly in the ground.

Another good place for an olitory is on either side of a front walk as a simple border. Guests are greeted with fragrance as they walk along the path to the front door.

FRAGRANT PLANTS TO GROW

CHAMOMILE is hardy enough in a moist climate to be grown as a lawn. Once established, it can be mowed in paths in a fragrant garden or be used to cover a bench bordered in stones.

CLOVE PINKS are the gillyflowers of Elizabethan times. These pink blossoms are the ancestors of the carnation, but much more fragrant. While it is difficult to find these—they have been replaced by the less fragrant dianthus varieties—they are well worth looking for.

CORSICAN MINT grows so close to the ground that it can be planted between paving stones. Its strong peppermint aroma is released in the air whenever someone walks on the stones.

HELIOTROPE is a low-growing annual with a sweet scent that pervades the air whenever it blooms. Since many of the fragrant plants have no blossoms or bloom for only a short time, heliotrope adds a welcome touch of color with its pink blossoms.

LAVENDER is a stately plant with gray foliage and intensely perfumed spikes of purple blossoms. It is a fairly hardy perennial.

© Joanne Pavia

Heliotrope perfumes the air wherever it is planted.

LEMON BALM is a low-growing perennial of the mint family. Although its leaves do not retain their fragrance when dried, lemon balm is well worth planting for the intense aroma of its leaves in the garden and its tidy growing habits.

LEMON BASIL has much smaller leaves than regular basil, and the plants are smaller as well. It has an invigorating scent that combines lemon with the tang of basil.

LEMON THYME is a variety of the common culinary herb, and it is also used in the kitchen. Less hardy than other thymes, it has the same compact growth and tiny leaves.

LEMON VERBENA has the only true lemon scent that remains when the leaves are dried. In a potpourri, it smells more like lemon than dried lemon peel. Although it will not survive a northern winter, it grows quickly and is worth replacing each year.

MIGNONETTE is a low-growing annual whose flowers are modest to look at, but extravagant in their fragrance. Its sweet, musky scent was popular in Victorian days.

MINTS of several varieties provide scent both in the garden and dried for potpourri and teas. Although spearmint is difficult to contain, it can be grown in a tub that is submerged to the rim in the ground. Or grow the intensely fragrant orange and eau de cologne varieties, both of which are slower to spread.

SCENTED GERANIUM plants come in a variety of fragrances, from a rich true rose to spicy cinnamon, ginger, and nutmeg varieties. Lemon is a particularly aromatic type that keeps its scent well when dried. These plants cannot be left outdoors for the winter, except in warm climates, but they make excellent houseplants.

Scented geranium plants add fragrance to any room in the house all through the winter.

© Sue Pashko/Envision

Spearmint should be grown away from other plants or confined to a container.

ROSES

Hybrid roses are larger than the old-fashioned June-blooming varieties and keep better in cut arrangements. But breeding to develop these qualities has taken its toll on their fragrance—or at least on its durability. While they are fresh, many hybrid roses are still strongly scented, and that sweet aroma will waft through your garden throughout the summer if you keep the faded blossoms clipped off.

You will, however, also want old-fashioned roses, the kind that grow wild along old stone walls on country roads.

It is for their fragrance when dried that the old rose varieties are most treasured. The aromas of *Rosa gallica*, *R. eglanteria*, *R. damascena*, and *R. canina* linger strongly when dried, and they are the preferred varieties as the base for potpourris. The colors remain, too, but will fade if the dried blossoms are exposed to sunlight.

Pick rosebuds to dry while they are still tightly closed and spread them on screens in a shady, airy place. For petals, pick when the rose is just fully opened, but before blossoms begin to shatter.

Roses are everyone's favorite scented flower.

© Lynn Karlin

Hybrid roses rarely retain their scent when they are dried.

Rose hips may be used fresh or dried for a tangy tea.

If the roses are not picked, most varieties will "bloom" again in the fall with a crop of scarlet rose hips, full of vitamin C and tangy flavor. Rose hips can be snipped off as soon as they turn red and used fresh to make jelly or syrup. Dried and steeped, they make a favorite pick-me-up tea.

The fragrance of the old roses can lend an incomparable flavor to foods. Use fresh rose petals in fruit compotes, or sprinkle them in the bottom of a pan before pouring in white cake batter. Spread a layer of petals in an apple pie before adding the top crust for a flavor combination discovered by the Shakers. Rose sugar for tea and baking is easy to make by layering white sugar and rose petals in a jar and leaving it sealed for a few weeks. If the moisture of the petals makes the sugar lumpy, break it up in a blender.

Roses are easy to grow, and the better nurseries, such as Jackson and Perkins Co., send complete care instructions with each bush shipped. In the North, hybrid roses may need some winter protection, such as a cap to shield them from the alternate freezing and thawing that breaks tiny root ends.

POTPOURRI

You will need to save and dry fragrant flowers, herbs, and leaves for your potpourri as they come into bloom. Nearly any flower or leaf can be a part of potpourri if it is attractive when dried. Along with those for fragrance, you will want colorful blossoms and larger blooms, whose main purpose is to create air spaces for the scents.

Plants with long stems can be tied into bundles and hung upside down in an airy, shady place. Hanging them inside a paper bag, as you would with herbs, will keep them clean and prevent losing little pieces. Since you won't need the stems in your potpourri, you can also dry single blossoms by laying them on a screen in a shady place until they are crisp. Store all dried flowers or herbs in bags or jars.

In some potpourris, you can add kitchen ingredients such as cinnamon sticks, whole cloves, and whole allspice. Be sure to save all your orange, lemon, lime, and tangerine peels. Cut them into strips and dry to add a citrus touch to floral potpourris.

The scent of a potpourri blend is not the only consideration. Color is important in a blend that will be displayed

Even the tiniest sprigs pruned from fragrant plants may be dried for potpourri.

in a glass or open container. Include plenty of bright blossoms just for their good looks. Bulk, as well as color, is provided by larger whole flowers, such as zinnias, marigolds, celosia, strawflowers, globe amaranth, delphinium, and statice. Some flowers, such as whole roses, provide color, bulk, *and* fragrance.

When the potpourri smells and looks right, its fragrance must be preserved and strengthened. Orris, the dried root of the *Iris florentina*, is the best fixative. It has no scent of its own but helps preserve others. Be sure to purchase orrisroot chips, not powder, which will give your potpourri a dusty look.

Drying evaporates some of the fragrant oils in flowers, but these can be replaced by essential oils. Rose is the most versatile of these oils and blends well with nearly any other scent. Lavender is the strongest and tends to predominate others. Bay, cedar, orange, lemon, gardenia, and carnation are also good additions, but since good oils are quite expensive, it is best to begin with one or two and add more if you find you enjoy the hobby. Be sure you are buying true oils, not artificial ones labeled "potpourri fragrance" or "refresher oil."

Mix your ingredients in whatever quantity you have or like, adding one or two tablespoons of orrisroot per pint. Mix the oil and orrisroot together first and then add to the flowers. Depending on the intended use for the potpourri, use four to eight drops of oil per pint of flowers. Stir or shake well and seal in a jar with plenty of air space. Shake or stir it daily for two weeks to allow it to blend and ripen.

Display potpourri in a jar or dish with a cover so it can be kept closed as many hours a day as it is open. Try to keep the blend out of the sun, which will fade both color and scent. If the fragrance does fade, simply treat it as you would a brand-new mix—add orrisroot and oil and let it blend in a large jar for two weeks.

While recipes aren't necessary—you can mix nearly any fragrant flowers and leaves for a potpourri—beginners may appreciate a few ideas to try. Add whatever else you have, leave out what you don't have, and keep experimenting to come up with blends that are entirely yours.

Small fabric bags can be filled with potpourri and used to scent closets and bureau drawers.

LAVENDER POTPOURRI

1 cup lavender flowers

½ cup roses

½ cup blue and white flowers

1 tablespoon lemon peel

2 tablespoons orrisroot chips

4 to 6 drops lavender oil

SUMMER GARDEN POTPOURRI

1 cup rose petals or buds

½ cup lavender flowers

½ cup lemon verbena

½ cup mint

½ cup scented geranium leaves

½ cup pink or white globe amaranth blossoms

½ cup blue statice

3 tablespoons orrisroot chips

6 drops rose oil

2 drops lavender oil

ROSE GARDEN POTPOURRI

1 cup fragrant roses

1 cup mixed pink flowers

¼ cup rosemary

¼ cup broken cinnamon stick

1 tablespoon whole cloves

½ cup broken bay leaves

3 tablespoons orrisroot chips

6 to 8 drops rose oil

THE PERENNIAL BORDER

Border gardens are a favorite showcase for larger perennial flowers. They have several practical advantages as well: They are easy to reach and keep up, they change with the seasons, and they can often be used to hide a foundation or wall.

Flower borders can accent a building or diminish it, outline a vegetable garden or a terrace, border a walk or driveway. They are beautiful beside a stone wall or lend a graceful crown to a retaining wall. If they have a fence, wall, and building as a backdrop, they are planted tall in back and short in front. By staggering the plants, you can keep them from looking like soldiers lined up in formation. If they stand free, bordering a drive or walkway, they are planted like the letter "A"—tall along the center and tapering toward the edges. Those gardeners with a flair for design will enjoy placing plants to provide contrasting colors of foliage as well as bloom. Others will choose the English dooryard garden style of exuberant abandon.

By alternating perennials with annuals and biennials, you can plan a first-year garden that is full and attractive, even though most perennials take at least a year to begin blooming and to fill out into lush clumps. Even after the larger plants have become established, you may wish to add some annuals for bright splashes of color and because they bloom for a longer period.

Spreading or very bushy plants are not the best choice for borders. Tall delphinium, foxglove, hollyhocks, shasta daisies, and phlox are best in the background, while pinks, zinnias, cornflowers, and calendula fill the center. Nasturtiums, French marigolds, sweet William, and silver mound artemisia often line the front in compact mounds that hide the stems of plants behind them.

The ends of a border can present opportunities as well as challenges. They are the place for large bushy plants such as baby's breath, as well as spreading clumps of daylilies.

While balancing the size and growing habits of the flowers, you also need to remember the seasonal nature of perennials. Each has its own cycle and its own timetable. The first spring blossoms are bulbs—crocuses that can grow right in your lawn and be mowed over later; tulips, whose foliage dies back in time to be covered with annual beds; and daffodils, whose clumps of narrow leaves can be braided and tucked under the foliage of later perennials.

Along with the flowering bulbs come the dainty violets and pasqueflowers. These are followed by irises, thrift, primroses, mallows, and yellow globe flowers, then by poppies, delphinium, foxglove, and achillea. Careful gardeners will also want to include some that continue to bloom through the fall—coreopsis, golden marguerite, coralbells, and basket flower.

GROWING PERENNIALS

Perennials develop more slowly than annuals, rarely flowering the first year. Once established, however, they bloom year after year, often expanding into showy clumps. They are usually started from plants, frequently taken from well-developed clumps by dividing the roots. It is important to know how quickly plants spread so you will know how much room to leave between them. Smaller plants set between newly planted larger ones can be moved to new locations as the larger plants spread.

Perennials usually bloom for a shorter period than annuals, so choose those which will flower at different times to keep a continuous succession of bloom. Don't forget to include flowering shrubs such as forsythia and azalea in your garden plan.

The soil should be free of weeds and grass and dug deeply for perennials, since their growth depends on a deep, sturdy

Hollyhocks are tall plants—a favorite choice in cottage gardens.

Nasturtium blossoms add vivid highlights of red, orange, and yellow.

Iris blooms early in the summer, shortly after the last tulip blossoms have faded.

© Joanne Pavia

root system. If the soil is sandy, add some organic material to help it retain moisture. Perennials will last for many years, so the time you spend now will save you time in caring for them later.

BORDER FLOWERS

BABY'S BREATH This perennial is white or pink with a cloud of tiny blossoms on a bushy mound. The plant usually grows to three feet and thrives in full sun. For drying, pick as soon as most blossoms are fully open and hang in a shaded place.

BEARDED IRIS This perennial is grown from rhizomes that should remain partially visible above the soil. The stately iris blooms in all shades from white to deep purple, including mauve and yellow. Blooms may continue for as long as four weeks in early summer.

DAYLILY This perennial is easily grown in sun or partial shade. It spreads quickly and is usually about three feet tall. It is very hardy and can be found beside old cellar holes where it has flourished without care for decades. Colors vary from yellow to orange.

Daylilies bloom continuously in midsummer.

DELPHINIUM This perennial comes in exquisite blue and purple shades, and grows from three to five feet tall in elegant spikes that may need staking for support. Its short blooming season in early summer can be extended by picking individual blossoms as they begin to fade. If none are allowed to form seeds, delphinium will usually bloom again in the autumn.

FEVERFEW A perennial of the chrysanthemum genus, feverfew will bloom the first year if seeds are started early. Clusters of small daisylike flowers on sturdy twelve- to eighteen-inch stems dry well for everlasting arrangements.

FORGET-ME-NOT This annual often self-sows in subsequent years. One of the earlier flowers, forget-me-nots will grow in sun or shade but prefer cool weather. They are very neat in the garden, where they are a favorite edging plant. Sow seeds directly in the garden in the fall in warmer climates.

FORSYTHIA A blossoming shrub, forsythia offers one of the earliest patches of color in the spring. Plants reproduce quickly from branches pushed into the soil and kept well watered until they take root. After its yellow blossoms have dropped, the forsythia is still an attractive though somewhat sprawling shrub.

GLOBE FLOWER This perennial grows in tidy clumps covered with bright yellow blooms. This old-fashioned plant blossoms early in the summer, long before most other yellow flowers. Its clumps may grow to two feet tall. It prefers rich, moist soil and thrives even in conditions of light shade.

© Derek Fell

Sometimes the delphinium blossoms of early summer are so profuse that their stalks need to be supported.

MARIGOLD This annual is easily grown from seed or purchased plants. The compact mounds are usually about twelve inches tall; colors range from yellows to golden russets. Marigolds thrive in full sun, but they do not require rich soil.

NASTURTIUM This is an annual grown from seed planted directly in the garden. The flowers range from pale yellow to deep red, and they bloom best in full sun with sparse watering. Nasturtium does especially well in seaside gardens and grows well in window boxes, where it trails nicely. Dwarf varieties usually grow in twelve-inch mounds.

ORIENTAL POPPY This perennial is tall with little foliage. It is one of the showiest and most dramatic of all garden flowers, but its glory is short-lived. A blossom may last only a day or two, so plant in groups for a longer season of color. Difficult to transplant once established, the Oriental poppy is best bought from a nursery where it has been grown in pots.

PASQUEFLOWER This perennial is among the earliest to blossom in the spring. Low-growing lavender flowers thrive along rock walls where they get good drainage.

PINKS These annual and perennial varieties are related to carnations. Between twelve and eighteen inches tall, they have pale green foliage and bloom in shades of pink, white, and rose. Even the perennial varieties will bloom all summer long if you keep the spent flowers picked.

SIBERIAN IRIS This perennial grows in round clumps of tall, graceful leaves. Its bright purple blossoms last well and bloom in midsummer, after bearded irises have faded. About three feet tall, the clumps are best for beds, not borders.

© Emily Johnson/Envision

Oriental poppy blossoms last for such a short time that it is best to plant a number of them for continuous display.

VIOLET This perennial spreads by self-sowing. Clumps of violets bloom in white and purple at the same time as daffodils, a very attractive combination, especially along a rock wall.

YARROW This is a perennial in bright yellow, red, and deep pink, about three feet tall. Large flat clusters will bloom for several weeks in summer if the heads are kept picked. It is a favorite for dried arrangements if picked and dried just before it reaches its full bloom. Clumps increase to create a showy display in a very few years; it thrives in poor soil.

YUCCA This perennial thrives in hot, dry climates but will do well in the North in full sun. Its showy clump of white flowers may grow on a stalk as tall as six feet, but its palmlike foliage is only about two feet in height. A dramatic plant for beds, it's easy to grow and very hardy.

Violets are a welcome early bloom in the spring.

A WREATH OF
PERENNIAL SEEDPODS

Unlike cone or herb wreaths, in which you must make the base of the wreath before you can begin decorating it, this wreath uses a purchased vine wreath. Vine wreaths are available from florist or craft supply shops or by mail. To decorate the wreath, use the seed heads and pods left in the perennial garden in the fall. Look for delphinium, Siberian iris, beebalm, Oriental and annual poppies, primrose, and black-eyed Susans. Wild pods and seeds can be added to make a more varied collection. Since there is no foliage for tucking in the stems, you will need a strong, quick-drying glue or a glue gun.

Lay the wreath flat on the work surface. Turn it until the heaviest portion is at the lower left-hand quarter. The bulk of the decorations will be on the upper right-hand quarter, so this positioning will provide a little balance.

Beginning with the largest, longest pieces, arrange the pods and stems along the upper right side of the wreath, extending them somewhat over the side. Lay sprays along the wreath facing both directions, with stem ends meeting at a central point. You can break or cut any stems that are too long and get in the way. When you like the arrangement of the longer material, glue the stems in place and add shorter pieces over the first group. Continue decorating the wreath in this way, ending with a cluster of short-stemmed seedpods in the center. If the pods do not offer enough color variation, add a few sprigs of pale-colored wheat or other ornamental grass.

© Lynn Karlin

Poppy seed heads are often used in dried arrangements.

CHAPTER SIX

A CUTTING GARDEN

Bright bouquets on the dining room table are one of the great joys of flower gardening. Anyone who grows flowers can enjoy this luxury, of course, but flowers suitable for bouquets are not always in bloom in the perennial border. Low-growing annual flowers such as marigolds and petunias do not work well in large arrangements. And, unless the ornamental beds are in the fullest of their season's finery, many gardeners hesitate to strip them of their bright blossoms in order to decorate the inside of the house.

Some of the best flowers for cutting are not especially beautiful in the garden. This is especially true of the flowers usually classed as everlastings, which can be dried for winter bouquets. Strawflowers grow on tall, rangy plants. Statice blooms in a blaze of glory, but it must be cut at its peak if it is to be dried. The tall silver king artemisia's tendency to spread, while not uncontrollable, makes it a difficult neighbor in a bed of mixed flowers.

The perfect solution to these problems is to plant a garden specifically for cutting. Such gardens are often at one end of the family vegetable garden, adding a colorful accent to the backyard as well. Flowers here are planted in rows, just like vegetables, so they can be watered and cultivated in the same way. With an abundance of annuals and no concern for the aesthetics of their placement in the garden, you'll always have plenty of available blossoms to gather into vases.

Here is the best home for giant zinnias, asters, spikes of blue salvia, and larkspur. This array of blossoms can be mixed with a few stems of perennials from ornamental beds or used by themselves to create arrangements. Those that dry well can be picked at their peak or just before to provide bright color throughout the house all winter. These everlastings are also the perfect addition to herbal wreaths and can be used for a variety of crafts as well as in fragrant potpourri.

Since the cutting garden is planted in rows and is not intended purely for aesthetic enjoyment in the field, the position of the plants doesn't matter. Most of the plants are tall, but you should be aware of the direction of the sun so that the tallest of them (strawflowers and sweet Annie)

will not shade the shorter flowers. Fortunately, the spacing between rows usually solves that problem.

If the cutting garden can be seen from the house and there are no other considerations, plant the lowest-growing annuals, such as salvia, statice, and gomphrena, in the rows nearest the house, the middle-height ones, such as giant zinnia, next, and strawflowers and the towering sweet Annie as a backdrop. This arrangement gives a stunning wall of color at the height of the season, when everything is in bloom at the same time.

Strawflowers are not especially attractive and are sometimes grown in beds alternating with other flowers.

© Mark E. Gibson

The easiest way to make an artemisia wreath base is to form it when it is freshly cut and still pliable.

FLOWERS TO GROW

ANNUAL STATICE Second only to the strawflower in popularity, this sturdy annual is available in beautiful shades of blue and purple, as well as pink, white, and yellow. Its stems are quite sturdy and hold their shape when dried upright. Be sure to cut statice just before it reaches full bloom to keep the colors vibrant. Although it can be hung in small bunches, statice crushes easily and is hard to separate when dry. Enjoy it as a cut flower by standing it in wide baskets and letting it dry upright. It will even dry mixed with other fresh flowers in vases of water.

ARTEMISIA Silver king and silver queen are tall branching perennials used for their gray-green foliage, which make beautiful bases for herb wreaths. They grow as tall as four feet and spread quickly from underground runners, so they are a good choice for a border along a fence. You can control their spread there and keep them in a perfect straight line by simply pulling up all the new sprouts early in the spring, which is the only time of year when they send out runners. Use these sprouted roots to extend the length of the bed or share them with friends. For wreath making, use artemisia while it is pliable.

BLUE SALVIA offers spikes of small blossoms that add variations in shape to flower arrangements. The color holds well when the plants are dried.

GIANT ZINNIA is the mainstay of summer bouquets. With plenty of room to branch out (room it seldom gets when used as a border plant), it will produce dozens of large flowers in a tremendous variety of colors. When buying seeds, look for mixed colors so you don't have a whole row of one shade. Smaller zinnias make good cutting flowers, too. Be sure to dry some of the beautiful heads for potpourri, since they keep their color well.

GLOBE AMARANTH is one of the lesser-known everlastings, with an abundance of blossoms that look like compact clover heads. They come in white, pink, orange, and rich reddish purples. If you pick off the first bloom of small flowers for potpourri, you will be rewarded with a hedge-like mound of large flowers that may be picked immediately or left on the plants for some weeks without deteriorating. Globe amaranth keeps its colors perfectly when dried, and takes up less hanging space if you strip most of the leaves from the long stems.

LONUS ANNUA has so many different names that it is best to check for the Latin name on the seed packet. It is quite small, but its heads of bright yellow flowers dry very well and can be wired to longer stems for use in taller dried arrangements. Seeds are not easy to find, but are well worth the search.

PLUME CELOSIA These feathery plumes come in a variety of vivid colors ranging from pale cream and yellow to deep russet orange and from pale pink to deep crimson. If the early annual flower plumes are cut off, the plants will produce subsequent crops of smaller heads on branching stems. While often used in borders, plume celosia intended for drying is better grown in the cutting garden.

© Anita Sabarese

Plume celosia's brilliant colors add interest to an annual border, or can be grown for cutting and drying.

Xeranthemum flowers provide delicate colors in dried arrangements.

A WINDOWSILL BASKET ARRANGEMENT

Narrow windowsills are not wide enough to hold flower arrangements, but are too large a space for miniature bouquets. This basket of dried flowers is designed especially for a shallow space. It would be just as attractive displayed on a shelf or mantel. The choice of flowers can change with the seasons or the color of the room. In a sunny window, gold and yellow flowers will retain their colors better than pink, red, and blue ones.

The container is a long, narrow cracker basket, designed for serving saltines. Into this, set a brick of Oasis or other soft floral base, cut to fit the basket.

Begin with large strawflowers on wire stems, placing them so that the center ones stand slightly taller than the outer ones. Bend their heads forward slightly. Add smaller strawflowers, with at least one trailing over each end of the basket rim. Fill in with statice and other flowers, such as *Lonus annua* or yarrow, keeping the design slightly higher in the center and lower at the ends. Fill out the arrangement with grasses and sprigs of sweet Annie, adding a few in the back a little taller than the rest and some longer curving ones trailing at the ends. These provide a soft frame for the flowers.

If the arrangement is a little top-heavy, secure it to the windowsill with a small strip of florists' clay.

© Anita Sabarese

Although yarrow grows in a number of colors, it is the tall yellow variety that keeps its color best when dried.

STRAWFLOWER Probably the best known of all the everlastings, these annuals grow on rangy plants as tall as five feet. Colors range from white and yellow to orange and brown and all shades of pink and red. It is usually sold in mixed flats. Dwarf varieties are attractive in annual borders or mixed with marigolds or zinnias. Harvest by cutting each flower head individually just at its base. Place on wire stems and dry standing up. The plant will continue to produce until the first frost.

SWEET ANNIE is one of the few drying flowers that retains its sweet scent. Tall spikes of soft green flowers also stay green if picked early. Picked later in the season, they turn a rich brown color. Either way, they are a special favorite of wreath makers where their abundant and fragrant foliage make a perfect foundation for arranging other decorative flowers.

YARROW The yellow varieties produce large flat heads of tiny blossoms on plants that may be three feet tall. Red and pink varieties have smaller flowers on shorter plants. All grow to mounds of fernlike foliage that spread moderately each year. Although yarrow is a perennial, it is so useful as a fresh or dried cut flower that you will want more than you can usually grow in an ornamental garden. Use it as a border to your cutting or vegetable garden, where it will create a "fence" of roots to help keep out invasive grasses.

© Anita Sabarese

A WILDFLOWER GARDEN

No gardener who has lavished care and attention upon flower beds can fail to admire the independent attitude of wildflowers. What people do for garden plants, the wildflower does for itself. It grows, blooms, replants its seeds, hybridizes, adapts to new climates, and thrives on its own, with a little help from the birds and the bees.

Self-seeding is not the most efficient of systems: A single plant may produce thousands of seeds in a single season, just on the chance that the wind will carry a few to open ground where they will gain a foothold. Inefficient as it is, nature's seeding works, as any gardener who has pulled out unwanted wildling weeds can attest.

But one person's weed is another person's wildflower, and some of the rangiest roadside weeds can enhance a garden if used right. There is a tremendous satisfaction in creating a landscape of native plants and knowing that you are helping to re-establish the balanced ecosystem of your environment.

It is important not to dig the flowers for your native garden in the wild. Many plants are not plentiful, and most are difficult to transplant successfully. It is better to collect their seeds and raise new plants or purchase clumps of perennials from reputable wildflower nurseries.

Ecological safeguards are even more important in the case of rare and protected plants such as the lady's slipper and trillium. Nursery plants are grown in a confined space so that the roots are not in such danger of breaking when transplanted. Unless you are saving native plants from the bulldozer, leave them in the fields and forests where they have already found hospitable spots and start new wildflower plants for your garden.

The most easily grown are the meadow flowers, those sometimes rangy flowers growing by the roadsides and in fields and pastures. They include daisies, brown-eyed Susans, wild iris, asclepias, asters, phlox, vervain, steeplebush, debtford pinks, daylilies, Queen Anne's lace, evening primrose, bluets, violets, and even the tall and elegant Saint-John's-wort.

Especially if you enjoy making dried flower arrangements, look for wild grasses and grains with interesting seed heads. These are often annuals, but they will self-sow. To keep them in place, cut the heads just before the seeds begin to drop, and plant a few of them where you want them to grow the next year. Clumps of these give attractive cover to the lower stems of the late-blooming, tall perennials such as asters.

While the seed catalogs are fond of showing entire fields of mixed wildflowers to tout their seed mixes, common sense tells us that this is seldom possible. Even though some seed houses package blends for separate climates, it is virtually impossible for a field or meadow planted with such a mix to produce anything near the display shown. Every new wildflower plant is competing with grasses and weeds that have been on the site for years. Established plants have strong root systems and are in their own best habitat.

If you do use such a mixture, rather than scatter the seeds to be lost in a field, prepare a smaller bed, carefully dug to remove weeds and roots. Install an edging that goes at least a foot deep to keep grass roots from invading.

Sow the seeds and cover with one-quarter inch of soil; keep the bed moist. The annuals will sprout first, along with any weed seeds that survived in the ground. Unfortunately, when you plant an assortment, you will have very little idea of what plants to leave and what to pull out until the weeds have gotten so strong a foothold that removing them also risks damaging your wildflowers.

For better success, spend a little more on single seed varieties and plant them in clumps so you will recognize them.

For a massed effect, try using only two varieties, such as Queen Anne's lace and black-eyed Susans, in beds at least two feet square. When they come up, you will be able to distinguish them from the weeds because there are only two varieties.

The meadow is not the only place to show off your sunloving wildflowers. Treat them just as you do cultivated perennials. Plant them, as the English do, along a fence or wall as a border or in freestanding flower gardens. Group them according to height, color, and blooming season.

© Lynn Karlin

Wildflowers are at home in very informal settings where they can spread naturally.

Along the back (or in the center of a freestanding bed), use New England asters mixed with Saint-John's-wort and Queen Anne's lace. Just in front, use clumps of phlox alternating with brown-eyed Susans, asclepiad, or wild iris. Hide the lower stems of these with clumps of ornamental grasses, and among those plant evening primrose, columbine, and vervain. Front plants could include pinks, violets, or cranesbill geranium.

These will bloom at various times. As you watch them bloom and grow over two or three seasons, you will move some, replace others, and add new varieties.

A Field Guide to Wildflowers in the Peterson's guide series is invaluable in identifying flowers as well as giving information about habitats. Before purchasing seeds or plants, you can check to be sure they will be at home in your garden.

However you choose to plant your wildflowers in planned or come-what-may fashion, you are sure to enjoy their colorful beauty. They have made themselves at home in our pastures, fields, meadows, and woodlands for centuries, and they are part of our natural heritage. Besides, when a stray wild weed sends its seed on the wind and it sprouts right next to your violets, you can pass it off as a lovely wildflower!

WILDFLOWERS TO GROW

BLACK-EYED SUSAN is the state flower of Maryland, but it is common throughout most of the eastern United States. Its cheery clumps of bright yellow flowers can be grown from seeds planted in late summer or fall. The plant will usually bloom the next year.

The delicate blossoms of Queen Anne's lace are lovely growing against a stone wall or fence.

© Anita Sabarese

Siberian iris forms a dark brown seedpod that mixes well with cones in wreaths and dried arrangements.

CONEFLOWER is a very showy perennial with purple petals drooping below a cone-shaped center. The cones remain after the petals have fallen and are used in dried arrangements. It grows to four feet in height and blooms in the summer.

LATE PURPLE ASTER is a joy for the northern gardener whose flowers are ruined by frost in the early September. It will survive in poor soils, even in partial shade, and reward you with a full month of deep purple flowers on plants about two feet tall.

PHLOX is available in many varieties, most of which have pink or white blossoms. Phlox blooms throughout the summer and grows from one to three feet tall. It needs some afternoon shade to do well in extremely hot climates but thrives in full sun in the North.

PINK COREOPSIS is a warm-climate flower that quickly forms a neat, low mat that blooms all summer. It withstands drought conditions easily and needs full sun.

PLUME GRASS planted in clumps makes a dramatic background in a large garden or a striking bed of its own. As tall as nine feet, it is topped with feathery plumes that bloom throughout the summer.

QUEEN ANNE'S LACE is a delicate white flower with feathery foliage. It provides a subdued look between showier or more brightly colored flowers and is a perfect border plant along a fence.

SUMMER-SWEET is no shrinking violet in the garden. It is usually at least three feet tall and may grow as high as eight feet. But its pink flowers last well and will spread to attractive clumps even in low, moist areas. Unlike many plants, it thrives near the ocean.

Although you should not transplant from the wild under normal circumstances, do watch for woodland areas that are being cleared for development. Ask the owners or developers for permission to remove any rare plants that will be in the path of the bulldozer. Take along large boxes, a sturdy shovel, and newspapers. Dig so that as much soil as possible remains around the roots, wrap the roots and soil well in newspaper, and place in boxes. Replant immediately, watering well for the first few weeks until the plants have settled in. Observe their native surroundings and try to put them in a location as much like the one they left as you possibly can, bringing several neighboring plants with them as well.

As you obtain plants, consider their height, and place them in groups with the tallest toward the back or at least separated by low ground covers. Ground-hugging species such as goldenseal may be used between clumps, but be sure these don't choke out other plants. Most woodland flowers are not grown for their masses of bloom, and they will look better and survive best if given ample room.

© Lynn Karlin

The centers of coneflowers are a nice addition to dried arrangements.

A WOODLAND PATH

Wildflowers are a particular favorite in shaded yards. So many of the common cultivated flowers require full sun that gardeners without it often give up. But some of our loveliest wildflowers are natives of the deep woodlands and their edges. Lady's slipper, trillium, mayapple, trout lily, bunchberry, Solomon's seal, and many others inhabit the deep woods natively, making them good choices for any shaded garden.

A woodland wildflower garden is easy to create in a deeply shaded yard or on the edge of a woodlot. Clear unwanted plants from the area beside the path, leaving as many species as possible. In most woodland settings you will want to leave most of the native plants, since they are the ones that fit into the local balance, but you can clear out patches here and there to make a place for rare plants.

It is a particular joy for the woodland gardener to be able to reestablish those flowers that were once plentiful in a locale. Trillium and lady's slipper once grew abundantly in the New England forests, along with trailing arbutus and others. But these have dwindled in number to the point where they are listed as protected species. By planting these, or other plants that have become endangered, in your own area, you can help bring them back to their place in the native landscape and ecosystem.

PLANTS FOR A WOODLAND PATH

BLUE PHLOX is a good ground cover for woodland gardens, where it spreads quickly. Its flowers bloom in the spring and early summer and, unlike most woodland plants, make good cut flowers for bouquets. It may grow as tall as two feet.

GOLDENSEAL provides a lush carpet, only a few inches tall. Its tiny white flowers and red berries are a good choice for ground cover between larger or more showy varieties of plants.

JACK-IN-THE-PULPIT blooms in the spring with a unique green and dark purple "pulpit" on a single stem. While it is not showy, it is attractive and one of the easier plants to establish. You can grow these from seeds if you gather them in the fall and plant them in a well-marked place. They will sprout the following spring, but blooms will not appear until the second year.

LADY FERN has lacy light green fronds that are the perfect backdrop for a woodland path. They grow to two feet in height and adapt well to any environment as long as there is plenty of moisture in the soil.

Choosing plants for a wooded area can be the most difficult challenge in gardening.

A BERRY BOWL

A popular item at garden club sales and church bazaars in the fall, these small bowls of woodland evergreens form a miniature environment that will last all winter. In the spring, you can replant the greens in your woodland garden. The container is a rose bowl, a spherical glass bowl with a small opening at the top. These are available at florist shops, but if you cannot find one, use a short kitchen storage jar with a cork top. You will need some small forest evergreens, live, with roots. Partridgeberry is the favorite, but goldenseal and checkerberry are good additions. The base is green moss with roots and soil attached.

Place the moss with its root and soil side up in the bottom of the bowl. Arrange the greens so that they encircle the inside of the bowl with as many berries showing as possible. Gently press the tiny roots into the soil. The bowl should be between a half and three-quarters full. If the soil or plants seem dry, sprinkle with a little water. Cover with a circle of clinging plastic wrap to seal in moisture, or with a cork seal if a kitchen jar is used.

Leave the bowl in a shady place for a few days. If moisture condenses on the inside, loosen the cover for a few hours to dry it out a little. If the top of the bowl has a lip or rim, you can tie a narrow red ribbon around it to decorate it and hold the covering in place.

Berry bowls stay green and healthy all winter if they are not left in the sun or allowed to dry out completely.

PARTRIDGEBERRY is a trailing evergreen with tiny round leaves of lustrous dark green. Its white blossoms hug the stems and turn into bright red berries in the fall. The plant continues to thrive all winter, even under the snow. If you find a large patch of this trailing plant and have the landowner's permission, take a few lengths of the runner and transplant it to your own woodland garden. It likes the same soil as pine trees and often hides under their fallen needles. Be sure the little roots are gently pressed into the soil, then cover the plant lightly with pine needles until it takes root.

SOLOMON'S SEAL is large and showy and as attractive in single plants as it is in masses. Its white flowers grow in pairs along an arching stalk in the spring and early summer, and its foliage remains attractive throughout the fall.

VIRGINIA BLUEBELLS add their lovely blue flowers to the spring garden. The flowers emerge pink but turn blue within a short time. After the plant blooms, its foliage withers and disappears completely until the following spring, so be sure to mark its location and avoid planting other things over it.

WHITE BEAR SEDGE, a broad-leafed evergreen, is native in many parts of North America. It grows to about nine inches tall and will spread to form a good clump in the first season. Its white blossoms stand out in the spring and early summer against its blue-green foliage.

WHITE WOOD ASTER is one of the few woodland plants that blooms in the fall. Its heart-shaped leaves are attractive in the spring and summer as a background for the earlier flowers. Aster blossoms are about an inch in diameter. They do not require total shade, so you could plant these along the edge of the woods as well.

CHAPTER EIGHT

A GARDEN FOR WINGED VISITORS

While most gardeners endeavor to keep critters, from crows to woodchucks, out of their cabbage, other gardeners are busy planting flowers that attract wildlife. Bees, butterflies, and birds—especially hummingbirds—are the chief quarry of these gardens, and the plants are chosen for their ability to attract and provide them with food and lodging.

Although bees, butterflies, and birds each have their own preferences and requirements, their needs blend quite well. You can plant a beautiful garden, your own little wildlife refuge, where these small winged creatures will feel welcome and safe.

You will achieve more than a pure aesthetic enjoyment watching the drifting butterfly and the hovering hummingbird in such a garden. By planting one, you are taking a positive step in preserving the natural environment and restoring the balance of its inhabitants. With increasing land clearing and development, such natural habitats are disappearing.

Even much of the land devoted to gardens might as well be a wasteland for all the support it gives native insect and butterfly species. So many popular garden flowers are exotics—plants that are not native to the place in which they are grown—that they are of little use to the native fauna. Some species are able to adapt to new food and nesting plants, but others are lost forever when their native "weed" habitat is replaced. The weed is some butterfly's nesting place or an important source of nectar to a bee.

Butterflies are attracted by the color of flowers, as well as by their scent.

One measure of a healthy ecosystem is the diversity, not simply the quantity, of its wildlife. The number of different species present indicates the ability of the environment to support its flora and fauna in good balance. Unfortunately, many plants that gardeners consider weeds and try to eradicate are important to this general balance, and the cultivated species chosen to replace them contribute nothing in return to the native fauna.

Your yard can become, or remain, a balanced habitat. By preserving as many native plants as possible, and adding those that are favorite food sources or nesting places for the bees and butterflies that help spread the pollen, you can make your yard into a haven—a rich, balanced part of the ecosystem.

For you, it will be filled with beautiful and colorful flowers. Butterflies and bees are attracted as much by color as by fragrance, both of which you can achieve through a steady succession of blossoming flowers. To choose the best ones, you must know a little bit about the habits of bees, butterflies, and birds.

Bees prefer yellow, blue, and purple flowers. They also need a quantity of the same flower, not just a single specimen. Massed plantings or large clumps of a single type of flower will provide them with more nectar than will a number of different flower species. While it is the color of the flower that initially attracts the bee, it is the scent carried back to the hive that tells other bees which flowers to look for.

Like the bee, the butterfly prefers purple and yellow flowers, or deep pink and mauve blossoms. The butterfly also needs a sunny spot, with no wind, for its perch. In addition to flowers that provide food for the butterfly, you need to consider plants that are favored places to lay eggs. Common milkweed, for example, is the favorite of the monarch butterfly.

Hummingbirds will feed on nearly any flower that provides a good supply of nectar, but they seem to favor those with a trumpet shape, such as trumpet vine. These flowers have such a deep tube that only the hummingbird bill can reach it, and they depend on this bird for fertilization. Orange and bright red blossoms rank highest in the hummingbird's preference.

A garden for bees, butterflies, and birds is not the place for extreme tidiness. What would be considered weeds in a formal flower bed are part of the garden plan here, and some of these creatures appreciate the cover provided by undergrowth that would seem untidy elsewhere. Save your energetic weeding for other beds. If anyone remarks on the resulting crabgrass that grows, just tell them it's a favorite resting place for butterflies!

Bees help spread pollen from plant to plant—a vital link for plant reproduction.

Butterfly weed got its name from its ability to attract the monarch butterfly.

While the form and design of the garden is not important to the creatures you hope to attract, its location is. All three need a sunny spot, and butterflies especially need protection from the wind. An unshaded spot facing south would be a perfect location, especially if a wall or fence faces the direction of the prevailing wind. Another windbreak possibility is an arbor. Plant trumpet vine or wisteria to cover it for a garden backdrop. A seat or bench underneath it can become the perfect spot from which to watch the activity in the garden.

Both birds and butterflies require water, so a small pool or birdbath would be a good centerpiece for this garden. This is not the place for fussy garden layouts; emphasize the wild nature of the garden. But do consider the height of the plants you use, keeping taller ones to the back and shorter ones to the front, so that you will be able to see and enjoy some of the wildlife you attract.

FLOWERS FOR BUTTERFLIES, BEES, AND HUMMINGBIRDS

BERGAMOT is so popular with bees that in some places it is known as beebalm. Butterflies will also frequent its pink and red flowers. It spreads quickly, so leave it plenty of room by planting annuals around it the first year.

BUTTERFLY WEED AND **MILKWEED** are members of the same family, as you can tell from their distinctive pods of fluff-born seeds. The blossoms of butterfly weed are a showy red, but its growing habits are more modest. It rarely reaches three feet in height, whereas the common milkweed often reaches four or five feet. Both are home to the chrysalis of the monarch butterfly.

DAYLILY blooms afresh each day and continues for several weeks. Give daylilies room to spread, and divide the clumps every four or five years. For variety, plant some of the hybrids along with the lighter-colored native varieties. Both hummingbirds and bees frequent them.

DELPHINIUM is a stately plant with tall spires of blue or purple flowers. Bees and hummingbirds seek its nectar, and its tall stems make delphinium a good showplace for the gardener to spot the birds. Plant delphinium near a window or along a porch or patio for a better view of hummingbirds at work. The stems may need staking to keep them upright under the weight of the flowers.

LUPINE offers a good breeding place for butterflies, especially in the northwestern states, and is a favorite of hummingbirds. Give the plants plenty of room, since they spread. Hummingbirds will be more attracted to the red varieties, butterflies to the blue, so plant both.

NASTURTIUM is sought by butterflies, bees, and hummingbirds for its sweet nectar. For the gardener, it is a useful border, with rich foliage and a profusion of blossoms. It thrives in the sunny location required by this garden and blooms better if the soil is not too rich.

RED SALVIA OR **SCARLET SAGE** is an annual wildflower that blooms abundantly throughout the summer. About two feet tall, its spikes are covered with brilliant color and work well in a massed planting. Start these indoors for a longer blooming period in the North. Hummingbirds can't seem to get enough of it.

VIOLETS are modest little spring flowers, which probably account for the term "shrinking violet," but both butterflies and bees seem to find their purple and white blossoms. They self-sow with abandon, but you can transplant the new clumps easily. They are especially pretty between the stones of a wall.

© Mark E. Gibson

Nasturtium attracts hummingbirds as well as bees and butterflies.

Small plants such as violets are likely to be overrun by the larger varieties in a wildlife garden.

CHAPTER NINE

A PATIO GARDEN

People without the space or time to grow a full garden have become so numerous that seed houses have developed strains especially for container growing. The availability of such tidy, compact plants has in turn encouraged more gardeners to grow vegetables in containers—even those gardeners with plenty of space for the conventional vegetable plot.

Container gardens have many advantages: no hoeing, little weeding, no strenuous labor, and easy mobility. But patio plants do need more attention than those planted in an open garden. Without deep soil in which their roots can seek water and nutrients, they must be fed and watered much more frequently. But for many, the convenience of having vegetables literally on the back porch, plus the attractive appearance of bush plants, outweighs the extra care required.

Choosing interesting and decorative containers is part of the fun of patio gardening. Clay pots, wine barrels, wooden planter boxes, window boxes, even large drain tiles make good planters. Porous material such as terracotta and untreated wood allow air and water to circulate easily, but they need more frequent watering. In hot, dry, or windy climates, nonporous materials such as glazed ceramic, plastic, or lined wood might be better choices.

Drainage is especially important; all containers must have holes or several inches of coarse gravel in the bottom. Setting pots on platforms helps air to circulate and protects patio floors from stains and puddles. Bases with wheels are easier to move if you need to follow the sun from one spot to another.

The second most important difference in growing patio plants is the soil. Potting any plant in garden soil is unwise, since its constricted roots need a richer soil with more moisture retention. Also, garden soil carries soil-born fungi, diseases, and insects that can quickly destroy plants in a limited environment.

There are excellent commercial potting soils available, or you can mix your own from equal parts perlite, vermiculite, and peat moss, adding one tablespoon of ground eggshells per quart of soil to counteract the natural acidity of the peat moss.

When digging plants from the garden to move indoors, you should first root prune them by running a spade down into the ground around the plant. Water the plant well and leave it in the garden for about a week so it can recover from the shock to its root systems.

HANGING BASKETS

Hanging pots and baskets bring dimension to a terrace or patio garden and attractive decoration to a porch. They are especially effective planted with trailing or cascading plants. If carefully planned, the pots may contain several different compatible varieties. Wire baskets should first be lined with sphagnum moss, then with a layer of black plastic punched with holes for drainage. Fill halfway with potting mix and set the plants in place. If you are mixing varieties, put an upright plant in the center and cascading ones to the edges. Fill the basket with soil, pressing firmly around the roots of the plants. Water thoroughly. Since wire baskets are open to evaporation from all sides, they need watering more frequently than pots.

Because of the water, these plants can become quite heavy, so be sure the brackets or hooks that support them are strong and secure. Rotate the planter periodically so that each side gets adequate sun.

Thyme, winter savory, and prosrate rosemary are good herb choices. Nasturtium is lovely with its mound of cascading foliage filling a pot. Some scented geranium varieties cascade well, and large-blossomed geranium plants are traditional decorations for summer porches. Bleeding heart, begonia, and impatiens also cascade nicely.

Geranium plants stay compact and full if they are kept well pruned.

Impatiens grow well in shaded areas.

While it may seem like a drastic measure, one further precaution should be taken when potting plants that have been growing in the garden—complete repotting in sterile soil. After assembling all the supplies for repotting, wash the plant's roots completely in a bucket of tepid water. Work the soil loose from the root ball with one hand while supporting its stem and swishing the plant about in the water with the other. Wash the foliage in tepid water as well, checking under the leaves for any pests or eggs that might be clinging to the undersides.

Fill a newly scrubbed pot about one-third full of dry potting mix and tip it so the soil lies along one side. Lay the plant roots against this soil and fill the pot, shaking it slightly to firm the soil and being careful not to injure the tiny root ends. An easy way to pack the soil snugly is to run a spatula blade down the edge of the pot and push the soil away from the edge with a prying motion. Then add more soil along the edge. Soak the soil thoroughly and set the pot in a shallow dish full of gravel so it can drain. If there has been considerable root damage, or the plant is very straggly at this point, prune it to encourage the development of more root and base growth.

Repotting takes a little time but saves you a lot of possible trouble later. Set any newly potted plant from outdoors away from other plants for a week or so to give it time to acclimate and to be sure it is not harboring pests that could start an epidemic. While it is not as essential to repot greenhouse-grown plants from a nursery, it is still a good idea, since you could be bringing diseases or pests into your patio garden, where plants have less resistance to them.

Many herbs make excellent container plants. Scented geraniums are frequently grown in pots, even outdoors. Bay and rosemary are often brought in for the winter. In fact, northern gardeners often leave these herbs in large pots year-round, setting them in the center of an herb garden or along a stone wall. Marjoram, thyme, lemon verbena, pineapple sage, chives, lemon balm, winter savory, and miniature basils do well.

Clay pots must be kept well watered to protect plant roots from dehydration.

© M. Long/Envision

Terracotta containers are available in a variety of interesting shapes and sizes.

Potted herbs, like all container plants, require regular watering, but they should be allowed to drain well afterward. Twice a week is usually about right. If they become too dry before that, perhaps they need a larger pot or soil with more humus content. Vegetables require more water, usually once a day, unless they get natural rainfall. Plants will need to be watered more frequently in hot or windy weather. Plants take both food and water through their roots, so a thirsty plant is also a hungry plant. Water each time until the excess runs freely out the drainage holes.

Unless they have full sun all day, patio plants tend to become "leggy" and may need to be pruned regularly to keep them full and tidy. Check the leaves carefully for any sign of disease or infestation, and treat plants to an occasional shower of soapy water if you find aphids or other insects crawling on them.

The location of the pots will depend on which plants you are growing. Conversely, the ones you will be able to grow successfully will depend on the location and exposure of your patio or terrace. With a sunny southern exposure, you can grow vegetables, herbs, and flowers. With afternoon sun in a western exposure, you can grow some vegetables, especially salad greens, and most herbs. If your patio is in the shade most of the day, you will be limited to shade-loving flowers, such as impatiens and begonias. If the pots are mobile, you can extend your sunshine by moving the pots from place to place, but that involves more work and, of course, being at home during the day.

Some seed catalogs have a separate page for varieties of vegetables, flowers, and herbs recommended for container growing. Look for these in the descriptions about each variety to see if the plant you like will thrive in that environment. Shepherd's Garden Seeds has developed a number of bush vegetable plants especially for this use. Tomatoes, peppers, lettuces, leafy salad greens, and even a bush cucumber are among the plants offered in the catalog.

Begonias can be used as standing or hanging plants.

Plastic pots can be set inside more unusual and decorative containers.

SOURCES

Alberta Nurseries and Seed,
    Ltd.
P.O. Box 20
Bowden, Alberta, T0M OK0
    Canada
*(Plants and seed, vegetables
and flowers)*

Andre Viette Farm and
    Nursery
Route 1, Box 16
Fisherville, Virginia 22939
(Hard-to-find perennials)

Herbitage Farm
Old Homestead Highway
Richmond, New Hampshire
    03470
*(Herb books and kits, Corn-
husk Doll Kit–Catalog $1.00)*

High Altitude Gardens
P.O. Box 4619
Ketchum, Idaho 83340
*(Flowers, vegetables, herbs,
and grasses for high altitudes)*

Jackson and Perkins Co.
P.O. Box 1028
Medford, Oregon 97501
(Rose specialists)

Johnny's Selected Seeds
Foss Hill Road
Albion, Maine 04910
*(Vegetable, flower, and herb
seeds)*

Native Gardens
Route 1, Box 494
Greenback, Tennessee 37742
(Native flowers)

Nichols Garden Nursery
1190 North Pacific Highway
Albany, Oregon 97321
*(Herb and flower plants and
seeds, vegetable seeds)*

Owens Farms
Curve Nankipoo Road
Route 3, Box 158A
Ripley, Tennessee 38063
(Trees, shrubs, perennials)

Potpourri from Herbal Acres
Pine Row Publications
Box 428
Washington Crossing,
    Pennsylvania 18977
*(Newsletter on herbs, fragrant
flowers, and everlastings)*

Robeson Farms
P.O. Box 270
Hall, New York 14463
*(Seeds for Butterblossom
squash)*

Rosemary House
120 South Market Street
Mechanicsburg, Pennsylvania
    17055
*(Potpourri supplies, catalog
$2.00)*

Shepherd's Garden Seeds
6116 Highway 9
Felton, California 95018
*(Unusual vegetable, herb, and
flower seeds, container vegetable varieties)*

Taylor's Herb Gardens
1535 Lone Oak Road
Vista, California 92084
*(Herb plants and seeds,
Catalog, $1.00)*

INDEX